Remember
You don't stop laughing because
you grow old, You grow old
because you stop laughing.

It has been said
"Laughter is the best medicine"
On that note, have a seat and
begin your treatment.

Rules are Rules

Hospital rules state that patients checking out must have a wheelchair.

One day a newly graduated nurse assistant came into the room to find an elderly man fully dressed. He was sitting in the bedside chair, with a piece of packed luggage by his side, all ready to go.

When he was shown the wheelchair, he was adamant that he was fully capable of walking himself to the parking lot.

But the assistant told him rules were rules, so he relented and let her wheel him out. In the elevator the assistant asked him if his wife was coming to meet him.

"I don't think so" he replied. "It takes her a while to change her clothes, so she's probably still upstairs in the bathroom taking off the hospital gown and getting dressed."

How OLD?

There was a man and a woman in an old folks home. The man says to the woman, I bet you can't guess what age I am.

The woman says I'll give it a go, but first pull down your pants, the man pulls down his pants, then the woman says pull down your underpants, so the man does.

Then she taps around down there and she says... you're 97.

The man asks, how do you know that?

The woman answers, because you told me yesterday.

Birth Control Pills

Mrs. Smith, an elderly woman, went into the doctor's office. When the doctor asked why she was there, she replied. " I'd like to have some birth control pills please."

Quite suprised, the doctor thought for a moment and then said, "Excuse me Mrs. Smith, but you're 75 years old. What possible use could you have for birth control pills?"

The woman responded, "They help me sleep better."

The doctor thought some more and continued, "How in the world do birth control pills make you sleep better?"

The woman said, "I put them in my granddaughters orange juice and I sleep better at night."

What is Celibacy?

Celibacy can be a choice in life, or a condition imposed by circumstances. While attending a Marriage Weekend, Frank and his wife Ann listened to the instructor declare, it is essential that husbands and wives know the things that are important to each other.

Then he addressed the men.

Can you name and describe your wife's favorite flower?

Frank leaned over, touched Ann's arm gently, and whispered, Gold Medal-All-Purpose, isn't is?

And thus began Frank's life of celibacy.

Homesick Snowbird

At The Villages in Florida last week, there was a bumper sticker on a parked car that read:

"I miss Chicago."

Someone broke the window, stole the radio, shot out all four of the tires, added an Obama bumper sticker and left a note that read:

"Hope this helps"

Doctors Referral

A doctor referral used to be a good thing...

...Now it means I'm too messed up for this doctor to handle.

- Bob Moher

Flawless Male Logic

Woman: Do you drink beer?

Man: Yes.

Woman: How many beers a day?

Man: Usually about 3 draft Bock beers.

Woman: How much do you pay per Bock beer?

Man: $5.00, (which includes a tip).

Woman: And how long have you been drinking?

Man: About 20 years, I suppose.

Woman: So a Bock beer costs $5 and you have 3 beers a day which puts your spending each month at $450. In one year, it would be approximattely $5400 correct?

Man: Correct. (continued) ▶➔

Flawless Male Logic
(continued)

Woman: If in one year you spend $5400, not accounting for inflation, the past 20 years puts you at spending $108,000, correct?

Man: Correct.

Woman: Do you know if you didn't drink so much Bock beer, that money could have been put in a step up interest savings account and after accounting for compound interest for the past 20 years, you could have now bought a Farrari?

Man: Do you drink beer?

Woman: No.

Man: Where's your Farrari?

[END]

BRAN MUFFINS

The couple was 85 years old, and had been married for sixty five years. They were both in very good health, largely due to the wife's insistence on healthy foods and exercise for the last decade.

One day, their good health didn't help when they went on a rare vacation and their plane crashed, sending them off to heaven.

They reached the pearly gates, and St. Peter escorted them inside. He took them to a beautiful mansion, furnished in gold and fine silks, with a fully stocked kitchen and a waterfall in the master bath. They gasped in astonishment when he said, "Welcome to Heaven. This is you home now."

(continued)

BRAN MUFFINS
(continued)

The old man asked Peter how much all this would cost. "Why, nothing" Peter replied, "remember this is your reward in Heaven". The old man looked out the window and right there he saw a championship golf course, finer and more beautiful than any ever built on Earth. "What are the green fees?" grumbled the old man.

This is Heaven, St Peter replied. "You can play for free, every day."

Next they went to the clubhouse and saw a lavish buffet lunch, with every imaginable cuisine laid out before them, from seafood to steaks to exotic desserts, free flowing beverages.

(continued) ➤⟶

BRAN MUFFINS
(continued)

"Don't even ask" said St. Peter to the man. this is Heaven, it is free for you to enjoy." The old man looked around and glanced nervously at his wife.

"Well, where are the low fat, low cholesterol foods, and the decaffinated tea?" he asked...

"That's the best part", St Peter replied, "you can eat and drink as much as you like of whatever you like, and you will never get fat or sick. This is Heaven!" The old man pushed, "No gym to work out at?"

"Not unless you want to", was the answer.

(continued) ➡→

BRAN MUFFINS
(continued)

No testing my blood sugar or blood pressure or...

"Never again. All you do here is enjoy yourself."

The old man glared at his wife and said, "You and your freakin' bran muffins. We could have been here ten years ago!"

[END]

If you donate your best suit to the poor, and they won't take it...

...that can't be good!

- Bob Moher

Cookies to Die For

A very old man lay dying in his bed. In death's doorway, he suddenly smelled the aroma of his favorite chocolate chip cookie wafting up the stairs. He gathered his remaining strength and lifted himself from the bed. Leaning against the wall, he slowly made his way out of the bedroom, and with even greater effort forced himself down the stairs, gripping the railing with both hands.

With labored breath, he leaned against the door frame, gazing into the kitchen. Were it not for death's agony, he would have thought himself already in heaven.

(continued) ▶——→

Cookies to Die For
Continued

There, spread out on newspapers on the kitchen table was literally hundreds of his favorite chocolate chip cookies. Was it heaven? Or was it one final act of heroic love from his devoted wife, seeing to it that he left this world a happy man? Mustering one great final effort, he threw himself toward the table. The aged and withered hand, shaking, made its way to a cookie at the edge of the table, when he was suddenly smacked with a spatula by his wife.

"Stay out of those," she said. "They're for the funeral."

[END]

Game Warden

A man was stopped by a game warden in Northern Algonquin Park recently with two buckets of fish leaving a lake well known for its fishing.

The game warden asked the man, "Do you have a license to catch those fish?"

The man replied, "No,sir. These are my pet fish."

"Pet fish?" the warden replied.

"Yes, sir. Every night I take these here fish down to the lake and let them swim around for a while. I whistle and they jump back into their buckets, and I take them home".

(continued) ➤——→

Game Warden
(Continued)

"That's a bunch of hooey! Fish can't do that!" The man looked at the game warden for a moment, and then said, "Here I'll show you. It really works." "OK I've GOT to see this!" The game warden was curious.

The man poured the fish into the river and stood and waited. After several minutes, the game warden turned to the man and said, "Well?"

"Well what ?" the man responded.

"When are you going to call them back?" the warden prompted.

"Call who back?" the man asked.

"The FISH."

"What fish?" the man asked.   [END]

Prescription?

A distraught senior citizen phoned her doctor's office.

"Is it true," she wanted to know, "that the medication you prescribed has to be taken for the rest of my life?"

"'Yes, I'm afraid so,'" the doctor told her. There was a moment of silence before the senior lady replied, "I'm wondering, then, just how serious is my condition because this prescription is marked 'NO REFILLS'.."

Waiting

The older we get the fewer things seem to be worth waiting in line for.

(Mostly because we forgot why we were in line in the first place!)

Missing Person

Husband: My wife is missing. She went shopping yesterday and has not come home.

Sergeant: What is her height?

Husband: Gee, I'm not sure. A little over five-feet tall.

Sergeant: Weight?

Husband: Don't know, not slim, not really fat.

Sergeant: Color of eyes?

Husband: Never noticed.

Sergeant: Color of hair?

Husband: Changes a couple times a year. Maybe brown.

Sergeant: What was she wearing?

Husband: Could have been a skirt, or shorts.

(continued)

Missing Person
(Continued)

Sergeant: What kind of car did she go in?

Husband: She went in a truck.

Sergeant: What kind of truck was it?

Husband: Brand new 2017 Ford F150 King Ranch 4x4 with ECO-boost 5.0L V8 engine special ordered seats and "Bubba" floor mats. Trailering package with a gold hitch. DVD with navigation, 21-channel CB, 6 cup holders, and 4 outlets. Added special alloy wheels and off-road Michelins. Wife put a small scratch on the drivers door. At this point the husband started choaking up.

Sergeant: Don't worry buddy. We'll find your truck.

[END]

Only in Florida

At a nursing home in Florida, a group of senior citizens were sitting around talking about their aches and pains.

"My arms are so weak I can hardly lift this cup of coffee," said one.

"I know what you mean. My cataracts are so bad I can't even see my coffee," replied another.

"I can't turn my head because of arthritis in my neck," said a third.

"My blood pressure pills make me dizzy," another contributed.

"I guess that's the price we pay for getting old." winced an old man.

Then there was a short moment of silence.

"Thank God we can still drive!," said one woman cheerfully.

... *THAT can't be good!*

When the Judge, greets you with,
Well Bob, what is it this time?...
...that can't be good!
- Bob Moher

When your most successful friend
is still sleeping on your couch...
...that can't be good!
- Bob Moher

Aging

Eventually you will reach a point when
you stop lying about your age and start
bragging about it.
This is so true.
I love to hear them say "You don't look
that old."

Hear me now?

Bob feared his wife Bertha wasn't hearing as well as she used to and he thought she might need a hearing aid. Not quite sure how to approach her, he called the family Doctor to discuss the problem.

The Doctor told him there is a simple informal test the husband could perform to give the Doctor a better idea about her hearing loss.

"Here's what you do",said the Doctor, "stand about 40' away from her, and in a normal conversational speaking tone, ask here a question, see if she hears you. If not, go to 30', then 20', and so on until you get a response" (continued) ▶——→

Hear me now?
(Continued)

That evening, the wife is in the kitchen cooking dinner, he was in the den. He says to himself, "I'm about 40' away, let's see what happens." Then in a normal tone he asks, "Honey, what's for dinner?", No response.

So the husband moves closer to the kitchen, about 30' from his wife and repeats,"Bertha, what's for dinner?" Still No response.

Next he moves into the dining room where he is about 20' away from his wife and asks, "Honey, what's for dinner?" Again No response. So he walks up to the kitchen door, about 10' away.

(continued) ➤⟶

Hear me now?
(Continued)

"Honey, what's for dinner?" Again No response.

So he walks right up behind her, "Bertha, what's for dinner?"

"For God's sake, Bob, for the fifth time, CHICKEN!"

[END]

If your dad is asking your "New" girlfriend to pull his finger...

...that can't be good!

- Bob Moher

Some people try to turn back their odometers. Not me!

I want people to know why I look this way. I have traveled a long way, and some of the roads weren't paved.

Say What?

A man was telling his neighbor in Coral Springs that he just bought a new hearing aid.

It cost me four thousand dollars, but it's state of the art. "It's perfect"

Really!, answered the neighbor. What kind is it?

Twelve thirty.

Ice Cream

A little old man shuffeled slowly into an ice cream parlor in Bonita Springs and pulled himself slowly, painfully, up onto a stool. After catching his breath, he ordered a banana split.

The waitress asked kindly, "Crushed nuts?"

"No" he replied, "hemorrhoids".

The Shoe Box

A man & woman had been married for more than 50 years.

They had shared everything. They had talked about everything. They had kept no secrets from each other except that the little old lady had a shoe box in the top of the closet that she had cautioned her husband to NEVER open or ask her about.

For all these years, he had never thought about the box. One day the old woman got very sick and the Doctor said the end was near.

(continued)

The Shoe Box

Trying to sort out their affairs, as most old people do, the old man took down the shoe box and took it to his wife's bedside. She agreed that it was time that they look inside the box.

When he opened it , he found two handmade dolls and a stack of money totaling $90,000. He asked her about the contents."When we were to be married", she said, "my grandmother told me the secret of a happy marriage was to never argue.

She told me that when I got angry with you, I should keep quiet and crochet a doll"

(continued) ▶───→

The Shoe Box
(Continued)

The husband was moved to tears. Only two dolls were in the box. He thought she had only been angry with him twice in all those years of living and loving. He almost burst with happiness.

"Honey," he said, "that explains the dolls, but what about all of this money? Where did it come from?"

"Oh", she said, " I made that selling the dolls."

[END]

If your retirement plan includes a panhandler course...

...that can't be good!

- Bob Moher

Old Washing Machine

A husband is walking behind his wife and says, "Your bottom is getting so big it is like an old washing machine."

The woman keeps quiet and keeps walking.

Bedtime comes around and the husband starts getting amorous.

Wife says, "I'm not starting the old washing machine for such a small load. You'll have to do it by hand!"

Good news...

The good news is, I've made it to my golden years.....

...the bad news is, there ain't no gold!

- **Bob Moher**

The good news is, I've made a lifetime of donations to Goodwill...
...the bad news is, Now I'm buying them back!
- Bob Moher

The Swimming Hole

An elderly man in Florida had owned a large farm for several years.
He had a large pond in the back fixed up nicely with picnic tables, horseshoe pits, apple and peach trees.
The pond was properly shaped and fixed up for swimming.
One evening the old farmer decided to go down to the pond and look it over, as he hadn't been there in a while.

(continued)

The Swimming Hole

(Continued)

He grabbed a five gallon bucket to bring back some fruit. As he neared the pond he heard voices shouting and laughing with glee. As he came closer, he saw a bunch of young women skinny-dipping in his pond. He made the women aware of his presence and they all went to the deep end.One of the women shouted to him, "We're not coming out until you leave!"

The old man frowned, "I didn't come down here to watch you ladies swim naked or make you get out of the pond naked."

Holding the bucket up he said, "I 'm here to feed the alligator."   [END]

The Villages

A little old lady was sitting on a park bench in The Villages, a Florida Adult Community. A man walked over and sits down at the other end of bench. After a few moments, the woman asks, "Are you a stranger here?"
He replies, "I lived here years ago."
"So, where were you all these years?"
"In prison", he says.
"Why did they put you in prison?"
He looked at her, and very quietly said,
"I killed my wife."
OH!, Said the woman. "So your single?!..."

Wal-Mart Greeter

Two elderly Wal-Mart greeters were sitting on a bench at the entry way in Bradenton, Florida., when one turned to the other and says, "Slim, I'm 73 years old now and I'm just full of aches and pains. I know you're about my age. How do you feel?"

Slim says, "I feel like a new-born baby."

"Really?, Like a new-born baby?"

"Yep, No hair, No teeth, and I think I just wet my pants."

If your identical twin is featured on "To Catch a Predator"...

...that can't be good!

- Bob Moher

Knee Pain

An old man limped into the doctor's office and said, "Doctor, my knee hurts so bad, I can hardly walk!"

The doctor slowly eyed him from head to toe, paused and then said, "Sir, How old are you?"

"I'm 98" the man announced proudly.

The doctor just sighed and looked at him again. Finally he said. "Sir, I'm sorry. I mean, just look at you. You are almost 100 years old and are complaining that your knee hurts? Well, what did you expect?"

The old man said. "Well, my other knee is 98 years old too, and it doesn't hurt!"

Just a Wee Bit

"An extraordinarily handsome man decided he had the responsibility to marry the perfect woman so they could produce beautiful children beyond compare.
With that as his mission he began to search for the perfect woman.
Shortly thereafter he met a Redneck who had three stunning, gorgeous daughters that positively took his breath away. So he explained his mission to the Redneck and asked for permission to marry one of them. The Redneck simply replied, " They're lookin' to get married, so you came to the right place. Look 'em over and pick the one you want."

(continued) ➤⟶

Just a Wee Bit
(Continued)

The man dated the first daughter. The next day the Redneck asked for the man's opinion.

"Well," said the man, "she's just a weeeeee bit, not that you can hardly notice ... pigeon-toed."

The Redneck nodded and suggested the man date one of the other girls; so the man went out with the second daughter.

The next day, the Redneck again asked how things went.

"Well, "the man replied, "she's just a weeeee bit, not that you can hardly tell,...... cross-eyed."

(continued)

Just a Wee Bit
(Continued)

The Redneck nodded and suggested he date the third girl to see if things might be better. So he did.

The next morning the man rushed in exclaiming, "She's perfect, just perfect. She's the one I want to marry."

So they were wed right away. Months later the baby was born. When the man visited the nursery he was horrified: the baby was the ugliest, most pathetic human you can imagine. He rushed to his father-in-law and asked how such a thing could happen considering the beauty of the parents.

"Well," explained the Redneck, "she was just a weeeee bit, not that you could hardly tell ...... pregnant when you met her."

[END]

Say What?

Two elderly people living in Ft Myers, he was a widower and she a widow, had known each other for a number of years. One evening there was a community supper in the Clubhouse.

The two were at the same table, across from one another. As the meal went on, he took a few admiring glances at her and finally gathered the courage to ask her, "Will you marry me?"

After about six seconds of "careful consideration" she answered "Yes". "Yes I will!"

The meal ended and, with a few more pleasant exchanges, they went to their respective places. Next morning, he was troubled.

"Did she say "yes" or did she say"no?"

(continued) ➤⟶

Say What?

(Continued)

He couldn't remember. Try as he might, he just could not recall. Not even a faint memory.

With trepidation, he went to the telephone and called her.

First, he explained that he didn't remember as well as he used to.

Then he reviewed the lovely evening past. As he gained a little more courage, he inquired, "When I asked if you would marry me, did you say "Yes" or did you say "No?"

He was delighted to hear her say, "Why I said "Yes, yes I will, and I meant it with all my heart"

Then she continued, "And I am so glad you called, because I couldn't remember who had asked me."   [END]

Ventriloquist

A ventriloquist is touring clubs in Florida. With his dummy on his knees, he's going through his usual dumb blonde jokes when a blonde woman in the audience stands on her chair and shouts "I've heard enough of your stupid blonde jokes. What does the color of a person's hair have to do with her worth as a human being? It's guys like you who keep women like me from being respected at work and from reaching our full potential!"

The embarrassed ventriloquist starts to apologize, then the blonde yells, "You stay out of this, mister! I'm talking to that little bastard sitting on your knee!"

Seenager

I am a Seenager. (Senior teenager) I have everything that I wanted as a teenager, only 60 years later.

I don't have to go to school or work.

I get an allowance every month.

I have my own pad.

I don't have a curfew.

I have a driver's license and my own car.

I have ID that gets me into bars and the whisky store.

The people I hang around with are not scared of getting pregnant.

And I don't have acne.

Life is great. I have more friends I should send this to, but right now I can't remember their names.

Disco

Husband takes the wife to a disco. There's a guy on the dance floor giving it large – break dancing, moonwalking, back flips, the works. The wife turns to her husband and says: "See that guy? 25 years ago he proposed to me and I turned him down." Husband says: "Looks like he's still celebrating!!"

Secrets

A husband walks into Victoria's Secret Store to purchase a negligee for his wife.

He is shown several possibilities that range from $250 to $500 in price — the more sheer, the higher the price.

Naturally, he opts for the most sheer item, pays the $500, and takes it home.

(continued)

Secrets
(Continued)

He presents it to his wife and asks her to go upstairs, put it on, and model it for him.

Upstairs the wife thinks (she's no dummy), 'I have an idea, it's so sheer that it might as well be nothing.

I won't put it on, but I'll do the modeling naked, return it tomorrow, and keep the $500 refunded for myself.

' She appears naked on the balcony and strikes a pose and another, then another.....

The husband says, 'Good Grief! "You'd think for $500, they'd at least iron it!'

He never heard the shot.

Funeral on Thursday at Noon

[END]

Diapers

I know some of you old folks have been wondering why baby diapers have brand names such as "Luvs", "Huggies", and "Pampers", while undergarments for old people are called "Depends".

Well here is the low down on the whole thing:

When babies crap their pants, people are still gonna Luv'em, Hug'em, and "Pamper'em.

When old people do it, it "Depends" on who's in the will!

Mary's Question

80-year old Mary burst into the rec room at the retirement home.

She holds her clenched fist in the air and announces: "Anyone who can guess what's in my hand can have sex with me tonight!"

An elderly gentleman in the rear shouts out his answer: "An Elephant?"

Mary thinks a moment and says, "Close enough!"

Old Buddies

Three old buddies were out for a walk.

Old guy #1 says, "Windy, isn't it?"

Old guy #2 says, "No, it's Thursday!"

Old guy #3 says, "So am I. Let's go get a beer."

Expectations

Recently I went to the doctor for my annual physical.

The nurse asked me how much I weighed. I told her 135 pounds. Then she weighed me and the scale said 160.

She asked me how tall I was. I said, "5 feet, 5 inches." She measured me and I was only 5 feet, 3 inches.

So she took my blood pressure and told me it was high.

"Of course it's high," I said. "When I came in here I was tall and slender. Now I'm short and fat!"

Driving Question

A woman in her 70s was driving with a friend. She went through a red light. The friend didn't say anything. But then she went through another one. The friend said, "Do you realize you just went through two red lights?" "Oh," she said, "was I driving?"

Lower Sex Drive

A 97 year old man goes into his doctor's office.

"Doc, I want my sex drive lowered!"

"Sir", replied the doctor, "You're 97. Don't you think you're sex drive is all in your head?"

"Your damn right it is!" replies the old man. "That's why I want it lowered!"

Good/Bad News

The doctor tells his patient: "Well I have some good news and bad news..."
The patient says, "Lay it on me Doc. What's the bad news?"
"You have Alzheimer's disease."
"Good heavens! What's the good news?"
"You can go home and forget about it!"

Benefits of Aging

*** There is nothing left anymore to learn the hard way.

*** Things you buy won't wear out.

*** You no longer think the speed limit is a challenge.

How Do I Do?

A well dressed, debonair man in his mid nineties enters an upscale cocktail lounge and finds a seat next to a good looking, younger woman in her mid eighties, at the most. Trying to remember his best pick-up line, he says, "So tell me, do I come here often?"

Benefits of Aging

*** Your investment in health insurance is finally paying off.

*** You can sing along with elevator music.

*** No one expects you to run -- anywhere

Lessons

A retired lady needed some extra cash, so she got a guitar and took some lessons. Then she learned some of her generation's favorite oldies.

Then she got herself hired by a nursing home to sing for patients by their bedside.

After serenading one bedridden older lady, she got up to leave and said, "I hope you get better soon."

The patient replied, "I hope you get better too."

Benefits of Aging

*** Kidnappers are not very interested in you.

*** Your eyes won't get much worse.

Senior Texting Code

ATD - At The Doctors

BFF - Best Friend Fell

BTW - Bring The Wheelchair

BYOT - Bring Your Own Teeth

FWIW - Forgot Where I Was

GGPBL - Gotta Go Pacemaker Battery Low

GHA - Got Heartburn Again

IMMO - Is My Hearing-Aid On

LMDO - Laughing My Dentures Out

OMSG - Oh My! Sorry, Gas

ROFLACGU - Rolling On Floor Laughing and Can't Get Up

TTYL - Talk To You Louder

Confessions

An elderly man goes into confession and says to the priest, "Father, I'm 80 years old, married, have four kids and 11 grandchildren, and last night I had an affair. I made love to two 21 year old girls. Both of them. Twice."

The priest said: "Well, my son, when was the last time you were in confession?"

"Never Father, I'm Jewish."

"So then, why are you telling me?"

"Are you kidding? I'm telling everybody!"

The Famous Man

On day a famous man went to a nursing home to see all of his friends again and see how they were doing. When he got there EVERYBODY greeted him [because, of course, everybody knows him]. One man he noticed didn't come up to him or say anything to him, so later he walked up to the man and asked him "Do you know who I am?" and the old man replied "No, but you can go to the front desk and they'll tell you."

Benefits of Aging

*** You can eat dinner at 4:00 in the afternoon.

*** In a hostage situation you are most likely to be the first one released.

What's in a Name

A retired couple had dinner at their friends' house, and after eating, the wives left the table and went to the kitchen.

The two men were talking and one said, "We've been going to a new restaurant and it's really great. I'd recommend it very highly."

The other man asked, "What's the name of the place?"

The first man thought awhile and finally said, "What are those flowers you send a woman you love? The ones with red petals and thorns?"

"You must mean roses," he replied.

(continued)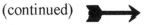

What's in a Name
(Continued)

"That's it," said the man. He yelled to his wife, "Rose, what's the name of the new restaurant we like?"   [END]

Late Night Lecture

An elderly man driving erratically was stopped by the police around 2 a.m. and was asked where he was going at that time of night.

The man replied, "I'm on my way to a lecture about alcohol abuse and the effects it has on the human body, as well as smoking and staying out late."

The officer then asked, "Really? Who's giving that lecture at this time of night?"

The man replied, "That would be my wife."

Magic Beer

A lady walks into a bar and sees a really-good looking guy sitting at the bar by himself. She goes over and asks what he is drinking.

"Magic Beer", he says.

She thinks he's a little crazy, so she walks around the bar, but after realizing that there is no one else worth talking to, she goes back to the man sitting at the bar and says, "That isn't really Magic Beer, is it?"

"Yes I'll show you." He takes a drink of beer, junps out the window, flies around the building three times and comes back in the window.

(continued)

Magic Beer

(Continued)

The lady can't believe it: "I bet you can't do that again." He takes another drink, jumps out the window, flies around the building three times and comes back in the window.

She is so amazed that she says to the bartender "I want what he is drinking." The bartender gives her a beer, she takes a gulp, jumps out the window, plummets 30 stories, breaks every bone in her body, and dies.

The bartender looks up at the guy and says, "You know, Superman, you're a real jerk when you're drunk?"

[END]

Romance

Karl and Ann were lying in bed one night. Carl was falling asleep but Ann was in a romantic mood and wanted to talk. She said, "You used to hold my hand when we were courting."

Karl reached across, held her hand for a second, and rolled over to try to fall asleep. A few moments later she said, "Then you used to kiss me." Mildly irritated, he leaned across, gave her a peck on the cheek and settled back down to sleep.

Thirty seconds later she said, "Then you used to bite my neck."

Angrily, he threw back the bed clothes and got out of bed.

"Where are you going?" she asked.

"To the bathroom to get my teeth," he replied.

Movies

An old man goes to a movie theater to see the latest action movie. After buying his ticket, he stopped at to purchase some popcorn.

The attendant says," $1.50 for the popcorn Sir."
"The last time I came to the movies, popcorn was only 15 cents."
"Well, sir," the attendant replied with a grin, "You're really going to enjoy yourself. We have sound now!!"

Benefits of Aging

*** Your secrets are safe with your friends because they can't remember them anyway.

Last Request

An old couple had four sons.The odd thing was that the older three had red hair, light skin, and were tall; while the youngest son had black hair, dark eyes, and was short. The old man eventually took ill and was lying on his deathbed when he turned to his wife and said, "Honey, before I die, be honest with me; is our youngest son really my child?"

The wife replied, "I swear on everything that's holy that he is your son."

With that the old man uttered a contented sigh and passed away.

As the wife wiped away a tear, she muttered, "Thank God he didn't ask about the other three!"

Getting Old When...

-Your back goes out more than you do.
-Your little black book only contains names ending with M.D.
-Your mind makes contracts your body can't keep.
-Your children are beginning to look middle aged.
-You sink your teeth into a steak and they stay there.
-Your knees buckle but your pants don't.
-You look forward to a dull evening.
-Everything that works hurts and everything that doesn't hurt doesn't work.

Viagra Please

One day an 80 year old man went to the drug store and asked for some Viagra. "No problem," said the pharmacist, "how many do you want?"

"Just a few," replied the man, "but can you cut them into four pieces?"

That won't do you much good said the pharmacist.

The old man looked at him sadly and said, "I am 80 years old, I am not interested in sex anymore.

I just want it to stick out far enough so I don't pee on my feet!"

Parking Problem

Johnny was driving down the street in a sweat because he had an important meeting and couldn't find a parking place. Looking up to heaven he said, "Lord take pity on me. If you find me a parking place I will go to mass every Sunday for the rest of me life and give up me Irish whiskey. "Miraculously, a parking place

appeared. Johnny looked up again and said, "Never mind, Lord. I found one."

Old is When...

-Going bra-less pulls all the wrinkles out of your face.

-You don't care where your spouse goes, just as long as you don't have to go along.

-You are cautioned to slow down by the doctor instead of by the police.

-"Getting a little action" means I don't need to take any fiber today.

-"Getting lucky" means you find your car in the parking lot.

-An "all-nighter" means not getting up to pee.

Older Lovemaking Tips

1. Put bifocals on. Double check that you're with the right partner.

2. Set alarm on your clock for 2 minutes ... in case you doze off in the middle.

3. Set the mood with lighting. Turn 'em ALL OFF!

4. Make sure you put 911 on your speed dial before you begin ... just in case!

5. Write partner's name on your hand in case you can't remember what to scream out at the end

Hospital Worries

"I'm so worried," the elderly patient said as the nurse plumped up his pillows. "Last week, I read about a man who was in the hospital because of heart trouble, and he died of malaria."

"Relax," the nurse said smiling. "This is a first-rate hospital. When we treat someone for heart trouble, he dies of heart trouble."

Getting Old When...

-Your new easy chair has more options than your car.

-You look both ways before crossing the room.

Patiently Waiting

A man called his mother in Florida. He said to his mother, "How are you doing?" She said, "Not too good. I've been very weak." "Why are you so weak?" "Because I haven't eaten in 38 days." "How come you haven't eaten in 38 days?" "Because I didn't want my mouth to be filled with food when you called."

Truth About Aging

-You can live without sex but not without glasses.

-You have a party and the neighbors don't even realize it.

Truth about Aging

-It's harder and harder for sexual harassment charges to stick.

-People call at 9 p.m. and ask, "Did I wake you?"

-You enjoy hearing about other people's operations.

-You get into a heated argument about pension plans.

-You know your old when people keep telling you how good you look.

-You're getting old when you wake up looking like your drivers license.

Parting Thought

When the husband finally died his wife put the usual death notice in the paper, but added that he died of gonorrhea.

 No sooner were the papers delivered when a friend of the family phoned and complained bitterly, "You know very well that he died of diarrhea, not gonorrhea." Replied the widow, "I nursed him night and day so of course I know he died of diarrhea, but I thought it would be better for posterity to remember him as a great lover rather than the big shit he always was."

Careful Now!

A funeral service is being held for a woman who has just passed away. At the end of the service, the pall bearers are carrying the casket out when they accidentally bump into a wall, jarring the casket. They hear a faint moan. They open the casket and find that the woman is actually alive! She lives for ten more years, and then dies. Once again, a ceremony is held, and at the end of it, the pall bearers are again carrying out the casket. As they carry the casket towards the door, the husband cries out, "Watch that wall!"

Medical Problem

An old woman came into her doctor's office and confessed to an embarrassing problem. "I do that all the time, Doctor Johnson, but they're soundless, and they have no odor. In fact, since I've been here, I did it no less than twenty times. What can I do?"

"Here's a prescription, Mrs. Harris. Take these pills three times a day for seven days and come back and see me in a week."

(continued) ▶—→

Medical Problem
(Continued)

Next week an upset Mrs. Harris marched into Dr. Johnson's office. "Doctor, I don't know what was in those pills, but the problem is worse! I'm doing it just as much, but now it smells terrible! What do you have to say for yourself?"

"Calm down, Mrs. Harris," said the doctor soothingly. "Now that we've fixed your sinuses, we'll work on your hearing!!! [END]

The Waiting Room

A patient goes to the doctor's office where, much to his surprise the doctor asks him, "Would you please help me with a problem I'm having?"

Sure, doctor, what can I do for you, says the patient.

"Would you scream in the most earsplitting, piercing screams you can manage? Try to make it sound as if you're in terrible pain." The doctor says.

(continued) ▶⟶

The Waiting Room
(continued)

"But why, doctor, you've always been gentle with me and your treatments have never caused me any pain?" Asks the patient.

"Yes," Says the doctor in a matter-of-fact tone, "but I have a 4 o'clock tee time at the golf course I don't want to miss, and my waiting room is still full of patients."

[END]

Thank You

Thank you for purchasing this book.

The average 4-year-old laughs 300 times per day, whereas the average 40-year-old laughs four times per day. A study done in 1999 revealed the average adult laughed 17 times per day when participants were asked to record how many times they laughed in three days

Please share these stories, jokes and quips with all your friends and keep the laughter going.

Thank You Connie Shipley for your help in completing this book.

Made in the USA
Monee, IL
16 June 2021

71498625R00046